T0030984

how we fare

ALSO BY MARY ANN MULHERN

The Red Dress

Touch the Dead

When Angels Weep

Sleeping With Satan

Brides in Black

HOW WE FARE

MARY ANN MULHERN

Black Moss Press
2016

Library and Archives Canada Cataloguing in Publication

Mulhern, Mary Ann, author
    How we fare / Mary Ann Mulhern.

Poems.
ISBN 978-0-88753-558-1 (paperback)

    I. Title.

PS8576.U415H68 2016

Editorial and Design Team: Jamie Adam, Alisha Adraktas, Maggie Chan, Hailey LeBlanc, Michael Mallen, Loren Mastracci, Amilcar Nogueira, Alisha Papineau, Sofia Tesic, Stephanie Voyer, Zoe Wilson

Black Moss Press

EST. 1969

Published by Black Moss Press at 2450 Byng Road, Windsor Ontario, Canada, N8W 3E8. Black Moss books are distributed in Canada and the U.S. by Fitzhenry & Whiteside. All orders should be directed there.

Black Moss Press acknowledges the support of the Canada Council for the Arts and the Ontario Arts Council for its publishing program.

Canada Council   Conseil des arts
for the Arts   du Canada

ONTARIO ARTS COUNCIL
CONSEIL DES ARTS DE L'ONTARIO
an Ontario government agency
un organisme du gouvernement de l'Ontario

PRINTED IN CANADA

PREFACE

In her novel *His Whole Life*, Elizabeth Hay writes, "gods descend and change things." In *Macbeth*, Shakespeare speaks of "the dart of fate."

Wars, plane crashes, tornados, Ebola, and gun violence end lives every day. The existence of loved ones is never the same.

Starting about three years ago, some local and world events struck me as more than yesterday's news. I saw poetry as a vehicle whereby I could create lasting images around school shootings in the U.S., forced marriages in Pakistan, solitary confinement, missing Aboriginal women, torture at Guantanamo, terrorism, and the like.

I met with Phil Hall, the Writer-in-Residence at the University of Windsor; he advised me not to editorialize but "to make the poem the event." This excellent advice gave me definite direction and permeates this collection.

It is my hope that the poems in *How We Fare* will influence attitudes, beliefs, and behaviours in positive, meaningful ways and allow readers to follow the light in unfolding the headlines.

Mary Ann Mulhern
November 2015

These poems are dedicated to the often forgotten victims and
survivors of every form of tragedy.
While reading this collection, keep the words of Issa in mind:
"In this world we walk on the rooftop of hell, gazing at flowers."

"Death twitches my ear
Live, he says
 I'm coming."
                    — Virgil

CONTENTS

EDITORS' NOTE

It should be noted that the headline at the bottom of each page indicates the article that inspired the poem. This is intended to establish the context surrounding the poem as well as to remind the reader that the images presented in each poem are rooted in fact.

BONES IN A BOX

My killer escapes these winter woods

His blade stained, sharpened with blood

Wolves smell fresh sacrifice

Sing praise to a red-rimmed moon

Drag me into their circle

Years before police toss naked bones

Into a numbered box

CYBERBULLIES

Two girls pick Taylor,

a classmate who

walks high school halls

alone.

They create a cyber page,

Taylor's face, a nude body

vulva and breasts exposed.

Students laugh

make lewd jokes.

The bullies boast.

She hides in her room,

covers her mirror in black

removes a small, silver watch

every minute pushes her

into a smaller, darker space.

The rope in her hands

twists into knots.

September 13, 2013 • Girl's suicide points to rise in apps used by cyber-bullies

FIBRES FROM THE PRISON TAILOR SHOP

Secrets wrap around my spindle

Smooth and tight, enough for fabrics of freedom

A prisoner branded with murder

Threads his needle with silk

Day after day, I teach him an ancient trade

Pattern, cut, binding, dart, and seam

His hands slide over cotton, linen, wool

Creases of flesh

My naked body in his midnight cell

He whispers his plan

How he'll loosen shackles of my marriage

Carry me to islands

Where rainbows gather jewels

Stolen from the sea.

WIFE NUMBER SEVENTEEN

My husband has twenty wives

Celestial brides blessed by God

He keeps menstrual charts

Horses and women, side by side

One night each month

A ritual of lust

My young body scrubbed

Hair tousled from ties and braids

Breasts released from bindings

into the grasp of hands

I know nothing of love

Every year my belly is heavy with child

Like the skittish mare

My husband tethers in a smelly stall.

DRIVE FOR FIVE

I stand before my team

Each girl mumbles her name

Defeat in eyes, shoulders, tone

As if I will forget every face

Place an X, black

My words challenge loss:

We will win, game by game

In five years, five national championships

Defeat is no compromise

We will win

Pub nights only on weekends

Summer holidays

Soft drinks, never

Practice daily, every morning

Athletic honour, always

I know how to choose recruits

Skill, stamina, passion

Shape of a team, belief in trust

Fervour of victory

We begin, keep on

A vision before us, constant

Each year a new world alive with light

Bright arms of the sun, a thousand cheers

Five years, five wins

Victory is the muse

Called Triumph

November 20, 2013 • Windsor Lancers' dynasty a product of coach Chantal Vallée's patience, commitment

FLIGHT 370

I am a passenger

In a tomb with wings

No Messiah to call my name

Lead me into morning

Rise of a scarlet sun

May 6, 2014 • Malaysia Airlines Flight 370 — only handful of subs capable
of hunting for jet

VULTURE

Sudan starves, parents and children, skeletal

A photojournalist hears whimpers

Sees a small girl, alone

Her struggle toward the feeding station

A hooded vulture shadows her, lands close, patient

Kevin Carter readies his camera

Captures famine, predator and prey

He chases the bird away

Watches the girl stumble, step by step

Why doesn't he comfort the child

Offer water, carry her, safe

How does a man become famous

When his muse has no name

Over her grave?

April 12, 1994 • Kevin Carter wins Pulitzer for photo from Sudan

SILENT LULLABY

She feared doctors, feared her father

Babies shaped from his seed

Dominique birthed each child, alone

Names would make them live

She gave them numbers, one by one

Buried two among roses, crimson, gold, ivory

Laid the rest in her garage

On cold nights she sacrificed sleep

Covered tiny bodies with a quilt

Tatters of her life

Courtrooms chant

 murder

Murder

MURDER

Sharpen the guillotine blade

A mother knows, children of incest

Cry in coffins, swaddled in darkness

Every heart, every door

Sealed with nails, tarnished, hammered deep.

June 26, 2015 • French woman on trial for killing eight of her babies

DETENTION CAMPS

Our bodies pile

Into temples of death

Hearts tortured for blood

Bones broken for sport

You wear masks and gloves

Pray

Light candles

As if the stench of flesh

Changes into fragrance

Sweet rise of incense

Bury us in fields of fire

Ghosts tend to gather

Where your children play

Whisper secrets

AN APPLE, SHARED

A girl holds an apple in her hand

Seeds of hope held within

Beyond barbed wire a starving boy stares

The girl tosses her apple into his grasp

In this moment both of them feast

A communion

here   now   forever

In years of memory he returns the apple

To his bride

She must be the girl

Who raised him from the grave

The one they called Auschwitz

Fed him fruit from the tree

Rooted in centers of Eden

ESCAPE

An old man believes

Home is there

Down the road

Past the nursing home door

Where mother stirs soup, bakes pies

Apple, cherry, and peach

He waits until dark

Shadows a worker past locks and alarms

Wanders into winter

A night too cold

Without coat, boots, gloves

He stops to rest near a ditch

Maybe it's warmer deep inside

Snow falling soft and white

Sweet as milk on his tongue

WITHOUT RESCUE

The boy abandons his Ski-Doo,

Begins to walk, surrounded by murders of snow

He believes in direction, the way the crow flies home

Night releases torment, wind and sleet

By now, his mother has called

For a search

In the twelfth hour he imagines an engine

Sounds of salvation from the sky

Everything fades into ice

The boy keeps on

An unnamed angel of the dark

Warms his young body

Bids him sleep in a downy white nest

No need for coat, hat, boots

Winter warbles her lullaby

He listens, lies down, silent

The moon watches from her cold circle

Enough light to keep vigil

February 4, 2012 • Military chopper used for Labrador fishing trip when 14-year-old Inuit boy dies on the ice

SPUN INTO A WEB

In grade ten

I knot a pink skipping rope

From the past

My life caught in a photo

Budding breasts in grade seven

Spun into a web

Where the spider waits

With a million eyes

Tweeted taunts of classmates

Texts to the little slut

Who stands on a chair

Kicks it into a grave

MURDER OF LIES

A boy speaks, murder of lies

His finger points to a cage

my name sealed in corners

How does a man breathe for thirty years

with only shadows to touch,

one gray blanket to warm an iron cot

Mine is an underworld Persephone has never known.

If a late spring opens prison gates

I will limp among strangers

An old man, blind to sun and stars

lost in numbered streets, new houses, dark windows

All of them locked.

November 1, 2014 • Innocent man released after thirty years

BEFORE

What happened before

The girl rode to the park

Before she left her shiny bicycle

On warm September grass

Before she slipped into the twilight

Of a sunset river

Could she take another breath

Could she rise

Swim back,

Pedal all the way home?

SACRIFICE TO EVEREST

We rise in the first hour

Brilliance of light over Everest

A legend we have come to learn

Rock, crevice, valley, ledge, and peak

The earth shudders

Our guide orders descent, immediate

Sun retreats from the roar of earth

I'm only eighteen

If Everest swallows me

I'll become a bone-flute

Echoes of my life

Played in the whim of winds

Forgotten in chaos,

Earthquake and avalanche

Burial grounds without markers

Names trapped in tombs

No one will ever find.

CHILDREN'S HOME

Nuns in white veils

Dress a Jesus child

Woven linen and lace

Lay him soft, gentle

In his manger bed

Down the hall

Orphan babies cry

Sin wraps them wet

In nights of Christmas cold

No sweet virgin

To suckle them warm

Sisters of Bon Secours

Lock the door

Pray for silence

June 7, 2014 • Bodies of 800 babies, long dead, found in septic tank at former Irish home for unwed mothers

NEVER ENOUGH GRACE

Foundations falter

Beneath the weight of walls and years

Gothic heights shiver in winds

Spawned in river depths, darker than any angel

Dampness, sharp as Satan's teeth

Sinks into bone

Seminarians, holy and not

Stroll lamp-lit halls

Cassocks and collars, rosary beads

Never enough grace for pedophile priests

Never enough forgiveness given

For those ordained in stained-glass splendour

Now silence as architects unveil perfect plans

Magnificence, visions of glory

Shaped from costs, millions

The bishop scans numbered ledgers

Brings an end to counselling for women and girls

Abused by hands anointed with sacred oils

October 30, 2015 • Bishop Fabro announces $30 million restoration of London's
St. Peter's Seminary

Leaves victims in shambles, shadowed with dust

To secure a future for seraphs and saints, blessed with light.

Silence.

HARVEST IN UKRAINE

A farmer witnessed children's shoes

Leap from the sky

All colours and sizes, some brand new

My child was on Flight MH17

Sandals packed in her new carry-on

She longed to stroll beaches of Bali

Leave footprints on sun-baked sands

The farmer will not step

Into a field of corpses and corn

Sunflowers that bow before the dead

Leave offerings of golden seeds

If only she would gather all those shoes

Late harvest of summer

Then I would have

something to hold

July 18, 2014 • Malaysia Air Flight MH17 shot down by missile, 288 on board

BIBLE STUDY

Like Judas at The Last Supper

I sit with the pastor, apostles

They welcome me

Young and white,

Eager to learn from scripture

Prophecies: Jeremiah, Ezekiel, Zechariah

Parables told by Jesus, my Saviour

This is their last hour, Gethsemane

I have shaped bullets into crosses

Nine black bodies crowd Calvary

Blood drips over candles

Darkens sacred texts

Words of Christ

Well done, good and faithful servant

June 19, 2015 • Nine dead in shooting at black church in Charleston, S.C.

33

THE FACTORY CLOSES

The factory closes.

First with words,

then bolts and chains.

Some workers pray

doors will open again,

most taste the sum of ruin:

dry swallow of nights.

The town veils itself

purple shadow of grief

as if there's a body

too heavy to bury;

decades of harvests

wagon-loads of ripe-red bounty

full-grown seeds

blackened with greed.

TRADED FOR SEX

Asha's mother weeps

this is the girl

who must go naked

into dark desert sands

search for an oasis

water to cleanse semen and blood

white flowers, petals to cover

a nameless shell

wind to take one last breath

STONING

The first rock exposes muscle, sinew, bone

Blood from her mouth darkens grainy sand

Her lover screams into the sky

God is not there

His word is in the stones

Made smooth in darkened depths

Sharia rivers, pious cleanse of hands

Prayers chiselled grey and black

Hurled into Heaven

Or Hell.

THE DEVIL'S KISS

In God is Our Light Church

empty seats accuse the pastor

who welcomed the sick

made the faithful lay hands

on faces swollen with death

All those bodies, buried now,

lips still parted in prayer.

Satan trespassed sacred space

embraced homosexuals, outcasts of grace

Ebola, the devil's kiss

stains every pew

clotted red turns purple.

AGING PARENT

Every day, my mother packs

A small case, family photos

Clean clothes rolled small and tight

One pair of shoes, her passport

She pleads with me, her only child

To book passage to China

To bring silk for a robe

White as the lotus

That opened on the pond

Of her father's garden

The morning she was born.

DOES GOD EXIST?

Theresa believed Jesus called her

To be his bride, to do his work

She washed bodies of old women

Left to die in the circle of rats,

Wrapped newborns in linen and wool

Baptized each child, waters of salvation, sacred

Young women followed Mother Theresa

Consecrated beautiful bodies

Poverty, chastity, obedience

Days and nights in hospice rooms

Comfort for souls in the breathless

Grasp of death

In the end, God withdrew

Kept his silence

Abandoned Theresa in deserts of doubt.

Visions of an oasis, luminous temples of grace

Too far

Maybe God was only myth

Words and dreams of old men

Stories scribbled in ancient sand

August 24, 2007 • Letters reveal Mother Theresa did not feel Christ's presence for last half of her life

ANOTHER SCHOOL SHOOTING

Like a dark ritual

From an ancient rite

A student enters his school

With a gun

Human sacrifice in hallways

Classrooms,

The cafeteria

He marks the last round for

Himself

Nightly vigils begin

Weeping, candles, hymns, and prayers

The light is gone

Buried in grassy graves

Names etched in whited stone

The gun, oiled and cleaned

Blessed

With bullets

WHEN WOMEN DRIVE

a car is like a lover

who takes a woman

from kitchen, cradle, and bed

through gates of cities

continents of ideas

oceans of thought

the slave who left the house

this morning returns

with a passport

no husband can burn

bury or weave

into a prison of veils

December 25, 2014 • Two women referred to "terror" court for driving in Saudi Arabia

CHILD OF GAZA

I might die today, tonight, or tomorrow

Caught like a mouse or rabbit

Between rockets of Hamas and Israel

Last week our house burned and fell

Rooms left naked, secrets spilled into streets

I look down at toys, blankets and shoes

Strewn about, lost in wreckage, war

My father and brothers are gone

When my mother lets go of my hand

I will kneel in the shadow of her soul

WRECKAGE

Our plane

Yet another body

In the scatter of branches

Broken

I am alone

Night all around

Like a wolf

Hungry

An owl calls

My mother said they bring death

Yellow eyes

Witness in the dark

I limp towards one dim bulb

My father's voice whispers from winter trees

"Keep on towards the light

Sanctuary"

January 4, 2015 • Miracle girl walks to a house after plane crash

GUNS AT SCHOOL

Classrooms fill with ghosts

Shadows of Christmas

Haunt spaces marked with blood

Angels sing in tatters of white

A tinsel tree shivers in dust

Scary spectre, a gunman

Armoured in black

Black wreaths on Newtown doors

Teddy bears line up

In drifts of snow

Like children on a field-trip

Still waiting for the bus.

TRAYVON

A boy walks alone

Purple shadow of a hoodie

A man watches, follows

Who knows what hides

Under a hoodie

Words are exchanged

Sounds of gunshot

Words die easily in the dark

So does a boy who is black

July 13, 2013 • Zimmerman acquitted in Trayvon Martin killing

BANGLADESH

Watch me feed yards

Of yellow, blue, pink, and plum

Into the spindle of profit

Tight weaves of greed

Pick a dark shade

Drape my bones

In Joe Fresh

Labels stitched inside out

Bind me into rags

Bright red dye

Long soak of blood.

LAST DAY OF SCHOOL

Tori skips away from school

Hand in hand with a young woman

Promise of a puppy

There in the car

Cuddled in the lap of a man

A friend

The door is open, honey

Fasten your seatbelt

We want you to be safe

WEDDING DAY

she's sixteen

ruined by a rapist

who has the right

to marry her today

in the next room

her mother stitches a white gown

the bodice

edges the skirt with hideous lace

the dress should be coarse

black

threaded with terror

laced with despair

hemmed with hate

in front of a mirror

the girl lifts her veil

poison from a metal cup

pours over swollen lips

every swallow

bitter

deep

at noon

the groom enters the house

his bride veiled

      silent

        cold

DESTINED

She's my Lolita

Destined for fame, Olympic gold

I'm the only one

Who can take her there

I know her centre of gravity

How her body is shaped for art

The perfect vault, beam, parallel bars,

The high bar

I've felt her tightness in every hug

How she craves my words, my praise

I've taught her how to kiss

Her tongue in my mouth, mine in hers

A secret

Soon, pink buds beneath her leotard

Will blossom in my hands

AT THE END OF THE RACE

I'm strapped into a chair

Wheels turned to a window

Above roads I used to walk, stroll, run

Paths that led to a room

Red carpet warm on my feet

A bed quilted with blossoms

Where I slept with you

READY FOR CHANGE

Like a Victorian schoolmaster

Stephen Harper stands behind a podium

Paints a black pall over the land

Without him in hallowed halls of Parliament Hill

There will be pestilence, terrorists in schools and coffee shops

Children born to misery

Hopeless

Justin just isn't ready

Nice hair though

Trudeau strolls among supporters, shakes hands

Poses for selfies, embraces infants, answers questions

His words shape the Canada we knew

Prosperous, safe, open to science

Channels of the future, alive with light

Free of Harper's Orwellian shroud

A bright red carpet spreads across every province

We welcome Prime Minister Trudeau

Justin's sunny ways

Nice hair too.

HOME

The house and I live together, abandoned

Fireplace of ash

A few candles, company of light

I'm in a small room, upstairs

Maybe a servant slept here

Or a child, unwanted

Winter scratches on glass

Wraps around my bones

Crows snatch sparrows in flight

Blood drips over ice

Machines plow across snow

No one knows I'm here

The house shudders, walls begin to shake

No one knows I'm here

HARVARD'S HOMELESS SCHOLAR

Teachers armed with red tipped pens

Label me, Toni Morgan: failure

I feel them inscribe my skin

Dig into heart and bone

I drop down

         Drop out

Failure darkens every thought, every page

Until someone offers light, encouragement

Words harbour warmth inside

A slow, clear radiance reveals

Who I am, who I can be

Something in my blood

Summons me back to books

TORTURE AT GUANTANAMO

If I tell you a naked man with broken legs

Stands all night on a filthy floor

Will you listen?

Will you hear

Echoes from Guantanamo

Scream across the bay

Cries of blackbirds, feathers rooted in blood

Caught in the whip of waves

Will you see the fade of stars and stripes

Necessary measures, security of our homeland

Safety, flap of words

Insane

TO RAPE A CHILD

Mama can't find me

Bones pulled apart

Blood in my mouth

Blood on my legs

Both dolls, dead

Mama can't find me

A man flees

From this horrible house

The key to the lock in his pocket

Is my five-year-old soul

I'll never get it back

SONY GAMES

A foreign comedy

Ready for release

Plots assassination

The American president

Poison in a breakfast sandwich

Memory slips

Body odour

Stumbles on steps of Air Force One

Hilarious

Flags appear across the USA

Crowds chant the anthem

Applaud cyber attacks

Calls for war

Stars and stripes darken screens

Silence words

Cancel every opening

Who owns freedom of speech?

December 25, 2014 • *The Interview* opens in US theatres

WEDDING POSE

like a summer swan

the bride poses above the waterfall

silk-slippered feet on a rock

beaded dress heavy with lace

veil dancing on air

photos for eternity

stolen from the flash of life

her lovely body begins to slide

fall

plunge into the gorge

torrents of water silence screams

her bridal gown a shroud

white absence of breath

pulls her into a grave

the camera continues to click

THE KISS

a young couple

leaves the game

lost Stanley Cup

crowds spiral

into shouts, fists, rocks

wild dance of fire

the girl screams

her lover covers her body

with his

kisses her mouth

a camera spins them

into cyberspace

young passion

awakens the globe

first breath of love

our bloodshot world

blinks

January 17, 2011 • Vancouver kiss couple were knocked down by riot police

CHAINED

Ordinary house, ordinary street

wallpaper rooms.

Ten birthdays wrapped in chains

A man who leaves rinds of food

Mouthfuls of water.

Whose seed swells in my belly.

My child cries,

Hinges on the steel door

Crack.

ISIS EXECUTION

A newspaper photo reveals Serbian soldiers

Reduced to underwear, bare feet

Marching over the red fire of desert sand

Some are only boys, barely eighteen

Silent

Mothers and lovers fold

Black and white print into palms of their hands

Memorialize the last moment

Hold the last prayer

One sweet taste of breath

The beloved, still alive, still whole

Before he kneels

August 25, 2014 • Captive Serbian soldiers forced to march to their
executions by ISIS militants

SOLITARY

At midnight I turn eighteen

If only there were a candle

Just one breath of light

To reveal I was ever here

I remember flowers

The wild ones: buttery, purple, pumpkin, orchid, white

How my hands yanked roots from soil

How blooms turned gray

A minute is an hour

An hour, a day

A day, a month

Alone, in this cell

Not even a spider, or a fly

Something

I can talk to.

SINS OF RESIDENTIAL SCHOOLS

silence

row upon row

faces slapped into stone

eyes like polished beads

counted on a chain

crush of mind, body, spirit

hawk and eagle hunt

over rivers, lakes, streams

seasons of fish and fowl

sacred creations the children learn

from their people, warriors and hunters

of earth and sky

medicine women and men

who grind roots, leaves and stems

ointment to heal wounds

the children suffer with Christ

mingle of flesh and blood

crosses in classrooms, over iron beds

carved from marrow stolen from souls.

January 3, 2014 • At least 4,000 Aboriginal children died in residential
schools, commission finds

FORGIVENESS WITHHELD

Father Sylvestre covers his face with a book,

Forgiveness

Fragile pages, faded print, gray

Steel bars of a Kingston cell tighten

Around his shrivelled heart

Death, early release

Too soon for reparation

The priest leaves forty-seven women

In shackles of his sins

Life sentences of shame

Bishop Fabro pleads for prayers

Victims in need of peace

Sylvestre's family, his name chiselled cold

The bishop makes an omission

A priest anointed with sacred oils

Passes into eternity

Without light, vigil candles

Intercession, rosaries, requiems

A grave too deep for redemption

GIRLS IN A SCHOOLHOUSE

In lonely hours of night

Mothers open books and backpacks

Their daughters' lives folded into headlines

Grainy photos, litany of words

Blood on a classroom floor

Coffins carried on wagons

Familiar grief, rain

The schoolhouse is a shadow

Over the patch of grass

Ghosts of five little girls

In white homespun dresses

Stand in line outside the door

Wait to trace their names

On a chalkboard, before they vanish

Into the silent drift of dust.

October 3, 2006 • Man shoots 11, killing 5 girls in Amish schoolhouse

HIS ONLY SON

An old man in Gaza weeps for his son

Eyes heavy with grief

As if they hold

The eternal sorrow of war

Blankets, books, clothes and shoes

Strewn in mounds of dust

Like the body of his child

Tossed into a crowded grave

Too many names to mark or carve

Not enough stone

LETTER FROM A DOG CAGE

caged like a dog

my naked body

a festered bruise

my stepmother shoves paper and pencil

into my cage

orders me to write down my thoughts

demands to know

why I still want to see my mom

no one likes me

why doesn't anyone

come to help me

when I die

                                        who will look for me?

MEN WHO TOOK TURNS

My naked body is garbage

Pitched into the street, filthy

A thousand footsteps pass

Six men who took turns

Under the two-faced moon

Made jokes

My small breasts, chapped nipples

Hair slicked with blood

How my womb broke open

How I spilled over their hands

CONVERSION

A young Muslim closes his Koran

Opens a bible

Moses   Jeremiah   David

And Jesus Christ

His brothers cry treason

Hunt him across borders

House to house

Habib kneels before a cross

Sees his body hung

Bullets in hands

Feet

And heart

If his brothers pitch him

Down rotted stairs

Or into a midnight street

Which god will claim his soul?

June 21, 2014 • A Christian convert on the run in Afghanistan

AT WHAT PRICE

a toothless Roma mother

dresses her children in gaudy rags

sells a baby girl

maybe the child will have food, clothes, books

safe shelter of care

maybe not

most of us wander into marketplaces

schools, partners, jobs

streets of what can happen

who knows the price

how we fare

CONTROLS OF MADNESS

Icarus shadows me

His wings

Feathers and wax

I carry weight

Passengers,

Burden of baggage

Descent is mine

Alone

The Alps

Frozen sea, rock and ice

White peaks reach up

Hands I must grasp

Ground control slices into silence

Shrill as a goddess

Jealous of my fame

This plane is mine

A gift to mountains

Where souls of Flight 9525

March 24, 2015 • Germanwings Flight 9525 passengers screamed as co-pilot crashed into the French Alps

Rise from blood and bone

Drift into whims of mist

Whispers of why

FLOWER OF FREEDOM

His flower of freedom needs

Twenty-seven years of darkness,

Roots alive with suffering

Limestone dust, limestone walls

Enough to blind the Sun

Mandela believes

There will be blooms

Seeds for generations

Brilliant showers of light

A rainbow.

LOVING HUSBAND

They say he sent flowers to her school.

Poppies disguised as roses

Savage tones of scarlet, startling as blood

Thorns alive on stems, thirsty for flesh

Every bloom open, ready for her grave.

Petals turn dark,

Cold in the clasp of snow

Leaves cling to stone yet to be engraved,

Her name, Nancy, dates of birth, early death.

No mention of murder,

Words too heavy

For the face of granite, veins of marble

Secrets her children must bury,

Frozen ground of years

A family marked by tombstones

History of whispers.

BLACK CARGO

Fear is the seabird above this crowded boat

His screams fall upon us

Like omens from an unnamed god

Water rises all around

Angry

Have we fled horrors of war

To become bait for sharks and gulls?

The boat drifts farther from light

Any harbour willing to take black cargo

Unwashed bodies

Souls with nowhere to go

May 11, 2011 • Libyan refugee boat carrying 600 sinks off Island of Lampedusa

CITY OF DARKNESS

Friday night in Paris

La Belle Équipe welcomes a crowd, noisy

Glasses sparkle, Chardonnay, Cabernet Sauvignon

Sweet bounty of Burgundy

Platters of greens, fish, and veal

Couples sway to

The sensuous embrace of song

Two gunmen darken the door

A volley of shots, marksmanship

We are only birds, resting from flight

Explosion of screams

The dead bleed into bedlam

My wife moans, agony of flesh, torn

We have one moment, hope of our child

I'll tell Tess to choose a star

The star of Halima, her mother

Follow the light.

November 14, 2015 • Owner of Paris restaurant attacked by gunmen mourns his wife, who died in his arms

MALALA

Words

Explode like bullets into blistered eyes

Of the Taliban

A child of fourteen refuses

To wander in a wordless desert

Without maps of the stars,

Guides to the moon.

Schools open to girls

A hired assassin

Aims for eternal silence

Malala's voice, the breath of morning

Echoes in the dawn

Freedom

ACKNOWLEDGEMENTS

About three years ago, I started writing poems inspired by news events. Marty Gervais, publisher of Black Moss Press, offered advice and encouragement. As the poems developed, Marty showed an interest in publication, for which I am very grateful. Phil Hall and Madeline Sonic, writers-in-residence at the University of Windsor, edited some of the initial poems. I deeply appreciate their advice and insight.

I want especially to thank "The Headliners," the editorial team headed by Marty Gervais. Their dedication, enthusiasm, and creative talent greatly benefited *How We Fare*. Members of the team are the following: Jamie Adam, Alisha Adraktas, Maggie Chan, Hailey LeBlanc, Michael Mallen, Loren Mastracci, Amilcar Nogueira, Alisha Papineau, Sofia Tesic, Stephanie Voyer, and Zoe Wilson.

Through Roger Bryan and the Odette School of Business, "The Headliners" connected with KPMG, a powerful source of marketing strategies. Early in the process, Brittni Carey conducted an excellent interview for CJAM Radio. Thank you all!

As a writer, I recognize the considerable talent of other voices required to create a book! *How We Fare* with Black Moss Press represents the very best coming together of hands, hearts, and minds.

Mary Ann Mulhern
January 2016